1 Introduction

In an industry with scarce capacity, a large firm may profit from leaving some of its capacity idle and holding output below the socially optimal level.[1] If rivals and potential entrants are capacity constrained, they will be unable to expand to offset the output restriction. This situation can arise for several reasons. Capacity may be limited by infrastructure, leaving individual firms with little ability to expand. The airline industry provides some examples.[2] Capital may be lumpy, or subject to large increasing returns to scale, making it uneconomical for an individual firm to expand capacity. Natural gas pipelines are an example. Capacity may be fixed by exogenous technical factors, as with radio spectrum. In all of these cases, there may be some ability to increase capacity through improvements in technology, but it is limited, at least in the short run.

Antitrust and regulatory authorities have historically been concerned with two types of market failures in industries with limited capacity. One concern is simply the welfare loss that occurs if one firm is dominant and restricts output. A second concern is that unfettered trading of capacity may place too much capacity in the hands of the dominant firm. Suppose that a dominant firm wishes to purchase capacity from a higher-cost fringe firm. Policy authorities then face a dilemma: on the one hand, society would benefit from shifting production to a lower-cost firm; on the other hand, because the dominant firm has market power, it may hold some of the acquired capacity idle and restrict output. Antitrust or regulatory authorities often block acquisitions by dominant firms if the cost savings are too small to counter the projected output restriction. This remedy is not ideal, as it prevents capital movements that would reduce industry costs, but it is a second-best solution if blocking transactions is the only policy instrument available.

A potential solution to both problems (distortions in the output and capacity trading markets) is to regulate prices, as was done in both the airline and natural gas industries for decades. In principle, price regulation prevents the dominant firm from restricting output;

---

[1]The first formal analysis of dominant firm behavior appears to be that of Stigler (1940). He showed that a dominant firm competing with a price-taking competitive fringe restricts output by an amount that depends on the elasticities of market demand and fringe supply.

[2]At many airports, capacity is limited in the short run by the number of runways and gates, although the number of seats on a plane is variable; airspace is limited, even in the long run. Safety considerations ultimately determine long-run capacity (given the infrastructure).

if prices are set correctly, it will also encourage trades that transfer capacity to the most efficient firms. However, price regulation has well-known shortcomings, and for this reason it is generally reserved for natural monopoly industries.[3]

An alternative approach is to pursue policies designed to increase firms' capacity usage directly. In this paper, we explore the welfare consequences of two such policies, one used by regulators and another used by antitrust authorities. First, in several industries with scarce capacity, regulators employ *use-or-lose provisions*, which require that each firm utilize a certain minimum fraction of its capacity. Use-or-lose provisions appear to address both distortions as they encourage dominant firms to increase output and they constrain output reductions following the acquisition of fringe capacity. Second, antitrust authorities often remedy potentially anticompetitive mergers by requiring the merged firm to supply or divest capacity to rivals. These remedies amount to use-or-lose provisions in which the usage requirement is imposed only on the acquired capacity and is fulfilled by the firms that employ the capacity after divestiture.

The history of capacity regulation in the airline industry sheds light on the issues surrounding use-or-lose provisions and provides the primary motivation for this paper.[4] Physical capacity limits the number of hourly operations at several airports in the U.S. In 1969, the U.S. Federal Aviation Administration (FAA) established the High Density Rule (HDR), which limited the number of take-offs and landings during certain hours at Kennedy, LaGuardia, Newark, Washington National and O'Hare Airports.[5] The HDR created rights to take-off and land—called "slots"—to allocate supply.

---

[3]Regulation of the airline and natural gas industries was widely believed to be counter-productive, so both industries were deregulated in the 1970s and 1980s. For a discussion of the problems associated with price regulation in markets that are not natural monopolies, see Breyer (1982).

[4]Many industries have been subject to use-or-lose provisions imposed by regulators, including the natural gas transmission, electric power transmission, wireless communications, and airline industries, among others. In the natural gas industry, Federal Energy Regulatory Commission (FERC) Order No. 636 requires pipelines to facilitate the sale of unused capacity. In the electricity industry, FERC Order No. 888-A indicated that if a customer withholds capacity with anticompetitive effects, FERC may require that the capacity be returned to the transmission company. The U.S. Federal Communications Commission (FCC) has enforced "loading" requirements for some wireless communication services to prevent hoarding of radio spectrum. For example, mobile radio operators faced a minimum use requirement per channel. (See 47 C.F.R. Part 90, 631 (Oct. 1, 2001).) Water rights, mineral leases, and fishing quotas have also been subject to use-or-lose provisions.

[5]See Federal Aviation Regulations Amendment No. 93-13, 33 *Fed. Reg.* 17896 (December 3, 1968).

The HDR initially allocated slots through unanimous agreement by a committee of air carriers. This system was cumbersome, and the FAA recognized that the committees were not "functioning in a manner which provides for the efficient allocation of slots for rapid adjustment to market conditions and shifting carrier needs and preferences, for adequate opportunity for expansion of operations, or for new carriers to serve high density airports."[6] In 1985, the FAA addressed the inefficiencies by adopting the "buy-sell rule," which allowed carriers to buy, sell, or lease slots, subject to a use-or-lose provision that required carriers to use slots at least 65 percent of the time over a two-month period or have them withdrawn and reallocated. The FAA adopted the rule "to permit maximum reliance on market forces to determine the slot distribution," stating that a benefit of the rule is that it "minimizes the need for government intervention in the continuing allocation and distribution of slots."[7] Regarding the use-or-lose provision, the FAA noted that most commenters supported the provision, citing the need to "prevent large carriers or several large carriers from 'hoarding' slots in an attempt to restrict service to drive up fares or to keep smaller competitors from entering into or expanding in certain markets."[8] In other words, there was concern that airlines might find it profitable to restrict their own output, or they might hoard capacity to keep rivals from expanding output.

In 1992, the FAA increased the usage requirement from 65 to 80 percent, stating that "[t]his higher percentage should encourage carriers to hold no more slots than their markets demand, potentially freeing up underutilized slots for use by other carriers without imposing impractically stringent use requirements."[9] The details of slot allocation rules have changed over the years, but the two essential features—slot trading and use-or-lose provisions—remain, as does the FAA's justification for use-or-lose provisions.[10]

Similar issues regarding capacity usage arise in the antitrust context. Merger guidelines in the U.S. and Europe discuss the potential anticompetitive effects of mergers when rival

---

[6] 50 *Fed. Reg.* 52181 (December 20, 1985).

[7] *Op. cit.*, 52184.

[8] *Op. cit.*, 52188.

[9] 57 *Fed. Reg.* 37310 (August 18, 1992).

[10] The 80 percent threshold remains in effect as of this writing. See 14 C.F.R. Part 93.227. In a recent Notice of Proposed Rulemaking for dealing with congestion issues at Chicago's O'Hare airport, the FAA stated that in the absence of use-or-lose provisions "carriers could hoard existing authorizations to increase the value of their holdings or simply to deprive competitors of greater access to the airport." 70 *Fed. Reg.* 15528 (March 25, 2005).

firms face capacity constraints. The U.S. Guidelines observe that a merged firm "may find it profitable unilaterally to raise price and suppress output," and that this effect is more likely if "rival firms face binding capacity constraints that cannot be economically relaxed."[11] Over the years, numerous mergers in both jurisdictions have been allowed to go through on the condition that the merged firm divest (or supply) capacity to rival firms, thereby offsetting the potential harm from the merger.[12] These divestitures can be thought of as use-or-lose provisions applied to the acquired capacity and fulfilled by the buyers of divested assets.

One possible drawback of divestiture remedies is that the divested capacity may be less productive in the hands of new firms than it was prior to the merger. For example, assets may deteriorate while divestitures are being arranged, the buyer may not have the information needed to employ the assets efficiently, or the merged firm may use an ongoing relationship with the buyer to limit the buyer's productivity.[13] A study of 85 merger remedies carried out by the European Commission (2005) found that only 56 percent of the divestitures were "effective" whereas 31 percent were either "partially effective" or "ineffective."[14] Further, it found that the divested business's market share fell in 57 percent of the cases, whereas it rose only 23 percent of the time. To the extent that divested capacity is less productive than it was prior to the merger, forcing a divestiture is analogous to imposing a use-or-lose provision.[15]

We study the impact of imposing a use-or-lose provision in a market with a dominant firm and a capacity-constrained fringe. To address the efficiency of capacity trading and mergers, we allow firms to buy and sell capacity before production takes place. Thus, we combine the restriction on capacity usage, which aims to expand output, with the ability of firms to buy or sell capacity, which aims to put capacity into the hands of the most

---

[11]U.S. Merger Guidelines, Section 2.22. See also EC Merger Guidelines, ¶34.

[12]See, for example, FTC (1999), Motta et al. (2002), European Commission (2005), and Papandropoulos and Tajana (2007).

[13]The latter may arise if there is a long-term supply agreement rather than a clean divestiture. See FTC (1999), Balto and Parker (2000), or Baer and Redcay (2000).

[14]FTC (1999) found that 28 of 37 divestitures it studied were successful in the sense that the divested assets created viable competitors in the relevant market. In the other 9 cases, the divested assets left the market.

[15]Both measures yield some output from capacity that would otherwise be idle, but less than the maximum possible.

efficient firms. To our knowledge, this paper is the first to study the welfare effects of using these policies together.

One might expect that imposing a use-or-lose provision would induce a firm with excess capacity either to increase its output or to sell some of its capacity in order to come into compliance, as suggested by the FAA. However, these strategies raise aggregate output and lower price. An alternative compliance strategy is to purchase capacity from the fringe and use it in production, thereby increasing the fraction of the dominant firm's capacity that is used. This turns out to be a more profitable way to comply with the constraint because it does not require an increase in aggregate output. Consistent with this logic, we find that the dominant firm is more likely to *purchase* capacity when a use-or-lose provision is in force. In fact, if the dominant firm and fringe firms have equal marginal costs, a use-or-lose provision will cause the dominant firm to purchase exactly the amount of capacity required to leave aggregate output unchanged (i.e., at the pre-regulation level). If the dominant firm has a cost advantage, then tightening the use-or-lose constraint induces the firm to acquire more capacity, which *reduces* aggregate output. That is, even though a use-or-lose provision increases the dominant firm's usage of any given amount of capacity, it induces the dominant firm to buy enough additional capacity that aggregate output *falls*. Total surplus may also fall if the dominant firm's cost advantage is not too large.

We do find one important case in which use-or-lose provisions benefit consumers—when the dominant firm is less efficient than fringe firms. In this case, the dominant firm has an incentive to sell capacity to the fringe in the absence of a use-or-lose provision. Although a binding use-or-lose constraint may induce the dominant firm to buy capacity, the dominant firm increases its output by enough to increase aggregate output. Total surplus may still fall, however, since output may be transferred from fringe firms to the less-efficient dominant firm.

Now consider a merger case in which a dominant firm has acquired capacity with the condition that some fraction of the capacity must be divested. The divestiture requirement will simply cause the dominant firm to acquire more capacity than it otherwise would, with the result that aggregate output is unaffected by the divestiture requirement. Now suppose that divestitures are less than 100 percent effective in the sense that divested capacity becomes less productive. Transferring 100 percent of the acquired capacity to the fringe, but having it generate only X percent as much output, is isomorphic to transferring $X < 100$ percent of the acquired capacity, but having it generate as much output as the other capacity. It follows that a policy of resolving mergers via divestitures of capacity may be ineffective if divested capacity is less productive.

In many of the cases in which capacity hoarding is a concern, there are multiple firms with market power. For example, many domestic U.S. airline routes are served by two large firms. This observation motivates an extension of our results to duopoly with a competitive fringe. We find that the qualitative results are similar to those with a single dominant firm. For instance, the firms are more likely to acquire capacity when there is a binding use-or-lose constraint than when not. If the constraint binds for both duopolists, and if the duopolists have lower marginal costs than the fringe, total output falls when the constraint is tightened. If both duopolists have higher marginal costs than the fringe, total output rises when the use-or-lose constraint is tightened. The impact on total surplus can go either way.

Capacity acquisition and use-or-lose provisions are the two essential elements of the current paper. Several papers have considered the impact of just one of these features. Capacity acquisition was the focus of Gale and O'Brien (2001), which studied a dominant firm and a competitive fringe producing in two markets.[16] The basic model of capacity acquisition and production parallels the model here, but the focus of the current paper is different because of the use-or-lose provision.

Krishna (1993) was interested in whether a dominant firm would outbid potential entrants for capacity that comes available exogenously. She found that the dominant firm would only acquire the last unit of capacity in a sequential auction against equally efficient entrants. We consider a one-time acquisition of existing capacity and get similar qualitative results if there is no use-or-lose provision.[17] Once again, the major difference is that we also consider a use-or-lose provision here.

---

[16]Some of the existing capacity was productive in both markets. The motivation for that paper was the Specialized Mobile Radio industry in which some frequencies were used for paging services but others could be used for both paging and cellular telephony.

[17]The dominant firm acquired the last unit in her model because of the discreteness of capacity.

Other papers have examined variants of the use-or-lose provision. For instance, Gale (1993) considered a *noncooperative joint venture*, which essentially involved a use-or-lose provision that required firms to use 100 percent of their capacity. (Rivals were permitted to use a firm's unused capacity.) We consider a range of requirements here (i.e., not just 100 percent), and sale of capacity is also permitted.

The remainder of the paper is organized as follows. Section 2 develops a model of capacity acquisition with a dominant firm and analyzes the benchmark case with no use-or-lose provision in force. Section 3 introduces the use-or-lose provision and examines its effects in both the regulatory and merger contexts. Welfare implications are investigated in Section 4. The case of duopoly is considered in Section 5. Concluding remarks are in Section 6.

2 The Basic Model

The market has a single dominant firm and a competitive fringe. The dominant firm has a marginal cost of c up to its capacity, k. Each unit of capacity enables a firm to produce one unit of output. The dominant firm is unconstrained in that its desired output is no greater than k. The fringe consists of a continuum of capacity-constrained firms with marginal cost equal to c_f up to their individual capacities. Fringe firms may vary in size, but each is small enough to be considered a price-taker. Aggregate capacity for the fringe equals f.[18] Inverse demand for the good is given by a strictly decreasing function, $P(\cdot)$, with a finite choke price.

The firms have the opportunity to buy or sell capacity before production takes place. We model capacity acquisition and production decisions as a three-stage game. In the first stage, the dominant firm announces how much capacity it wishes to buy or sell. Next, the fringe firms decide individually whether to trade with the dominant firm at the market-clearing price for capacity.[19] Finally, in the third stage, the dominant firm and the fringe

---

[18]We will implicitly assume that f is large enough that there is an interior solution in the capacity acquisition game.

[19]Instead of imposing market-clearing as the condition for determining price, we could allow fringe firms to receive individual offers and decide unilaterally whether to accept or reject them. In this model, one can show that if each fringe firm observes the total mass of firms receiving offers, then any perfect Bayesian

firms choose their outputs.

We look for a subgame-perfect Nash equilibrium. At the production stage, the dominant firm will choose a quantity to maximize its profit, given the fringe output. Fringe behavior is straightforward since it is optimal to produce up to capacity as long as the output price exceeds c_f (which we assume) since the fringe firms are price-takers. At the acquisition stages, purchase or sale decisions and acceptance decisions must be optimal, given the anticipated behavior at subsequent stages.

2.1 The Benchmark Case

We begin the analysis with the benchmark case in which there is no use-or-lose provision. This case provides context and motivation for the imposition of a use-or-lose provision, and it also provides the equilibrium characterization for cases in which the use-or-lose provision does not bind.

Let x denote the dominant firm's (net) purchase of capacity from the fringe. The firm's profit from production is then

$$\pi(x) \equiv \max_{0 \leq q \leq k+x} P(q + f - x)q - cq, \tag{1}$$

since the fringe will produce $f - x$. The following assumption guarantees that the profit-maximizing quantity is unique.

Assumption 1 $P(q + f - x)q - cq$ is strictly quasi-concave for $q \in (0, k + x)$, given $x \in (-k, f)$.

This assumption, which holds if the firm's marginal revenue is strictly decreasing, ensures that the dominant firm's profit function is single-peaked for any level of capacity acquisition.

The first-order condition for an interior solution takes the form

$$P'(q + f - x)q + P(q + f - x) - c = 0, \tag{2}$$

equilibrium yields the market-clearing price for capacity. See Gale and O'Brien (2001), Lemma 1.

9

for given x.[20] The second-order necessary condition is:

$$P''(q + f - x)q + 2P'(q + f - x) \leq 0. \tag{3}$$

Given Assumption 1, (3) will be satisfied with a strict inequality when q satisfies (2). Let $q(x)$ denote the profit-maximizing quantity.

To see how $q(x)$ depends on x, differentiate the first-order condition with respect to x. This yields

$$q'(x) = \frac{P''(q + f - x)q + P'(q + f - x)}{P''(q + f - x)q + 2P'(q + f - x)} = 1 - \frac{P'(q + f - x)}{P''(q + f - x)q + 2P'(q + f - x)}.$$

The denominator is negative so $q'(x) < 1$.[21] If the dominant firm acquires one additional unit of capacity, it will use the fraction $q'(x) < 1$ and leave the remaining $1 - q'(x)$ idle.

Now turn to the acquisition stage, and consider the relationship between the acquisition price and the amount of capacity acquired. The dominant firm announces the quantity that it will buy or sell. The fringe firms then decide individually whether to trade with the dominant firm.

Suppose that the dominant firm acquires x units of capacity from the fringe. Aggregate output will then be $q(x) + f - x$. Let $b(x) \equiv P(q(x) + f - x) - c_f$ be the price-cost margin of a fringe firm when the dominant firm acquires x units of capacity and then produces optimally. We now show that $b(\cdot)$ is the acquisition price for capacity, which means that larger acquisitions result in a higher price for output.[22]

LEMMA 1. *If the dominant firm submits an order for x^* units of capacity, the market-clearing price is $b(x^*)$.*

Proof. Suppose that the dominant firm submits an order for (and purchases) $x^* > 0$. The resulting profit in the production game for a fringe firm with a unit of capacity is $b(x^*)$. Thus, if the price of capacity were $b < b(x^*)$, those firms that sold would have been better

---

[20]We assume that the dominant firm does not end up constrained, which means that it does not *sell* a large amount of capacity. As we will see below, the dominant firm would only sell a large amount of capacity if the fringe were much more efficient.

[21]When it will not cause confusion, we suppress the arguments of functions such as $q(x)$.

[22]Since $b'(x) = P'(q(x) + f - x)[q'(x) - 1]$, the sign of $b'(x)$ is the same as the sign of $1 - q'(x)$, which is strictly positive.

off not selling. Conversely, if the price were $b > b(x^*)$, those that did not sell would have been better off selling. Finally, the fringe firms are indifferent if $b = b(x^*)$. It follows that the dominant firm will pay a price of $b(x^*)$ per unit if it submits an order for $x^* > 0$ units. The analogous arguments go through if the dominant firm sells capacity, so the analysis applies to $x^* < 0$ as well. **Q.E.D.**

Let

$$\Phi(x) \equiv \pi(x) - b(x)x = [P(q(x) + f - x) - c](q(x) - x) + (c_f - c)x \tag{4}$$

denote the dominant firm's profit from acquiring x units at the market-clearing price and then selecting the profit-maximizing output.[23] The capacity acquisition problem amounts to the following:

$$\max_{-k \leq x \leq f} \Phi(x). \tag{5}$$

We make one additional assumption.

Assumption 2 The profit from capacity acquisition, $\Phi(x)$, is strictly quasi-concave.[24]

Henceforth, we assume that Assumptions 1-2 hold.

The rate of change of the profit from capacity acquisition is

$$\Phi'(x) = \pi'(x) - b(x) - b'(x)x. \tag{6}$$

Using (4) and the first-order condition for production, (2), we can express the first-order condition for capacity acquisition as

$$\Phi'(x) = [1 - q'(x)]P'(q(x) + f - x)x + c_f - c = 0. \tag{7}$$

PROPOSITION 1. *(Gale and O'Brien, 2001). The dominant firm buys (sells) capacity if its marginal cost of production is lower (higher) than the fringe firms'. If marginal costs are equal, no capacity is traded.*

---

[23]We are implicitly assuming that the dominant firm will only acquire capacity once. It is conceivable that, having made a single purchase at $b(x)$, the firm would have an incentive to purchase again. If fringe firms anticipate this, they will not sell at $b(x)$ initially. The dominant firm could commit not to purchase again by using a most-favored customer clause. Alternatively, one could construct a dynamic equilibrium analogous to that in Ausubel and Deneckere (1989), where a seller lacking commitment gets essentially the same profit as with commitment.

[24]If $P(\cdot)$ is linear, for example, $\Phi(\cdot)$ is strictly *concave*.

Proof. Using $\Phi'(x)$ from (7) and evaluating at $x = 0$, we see that $\Phi'(0) > \ (<) \ 0$ if $c_f > \ (<) \ c$, and $\Phi'(0) = 0$ if $c_f = c$. The result then follows from the strict quasi-concavity of Φ. **Q.E.D.**

To get some intuition, suppose that marginal costs are equal. Now suppose the dominant firm purchases one unit of capacity ($x = 1$). The firm will turn q' into production and hold $1 - q'$ idle. Consider the costs and benefits associated with those two quantities. The cost of acquiring the q' units is $(P - c_f)q' = (P - c)q'$, since the price of capacity is the fringe margin and marginal costs are equal. The benefit from the q' units of production is also $(P - c)q'$, since the dominant firm earns $P - c$ on each unit sold. Thus, the cost and benefit of buying and using the q' units balance out. The cost of acquiring the $1 - q'$ units that will be held idle is $(P - c)[1 - q']$, and the benefit is $-P'q[1 - q']$, the additional revenue from the inframarginal units of output, which results from lowering aggregate output by $1 - q'$. This cost and benefit also cancel out because the original quantity was chosen to maximize the dominant firm's profits so a marginal reduction in q has no first-order effect. (Formally, the net effect is $-(P + P'q - c)[1 - q'] = 0$.) Putting these arguments together, the dominant firm receives no first-order gain from buying a unit of capacity and holding $1 - q'$ idle.

If $c_f \neq c$, the dominant firm will buy or sell. A rise in c_f lowers the acquisition price, all else equal. Thus, a dominant firm that is more efficient than the fringe will buy capacity. Conversely, a less-efficient dominant firm will sell.

One of the rationales for employing use-or-lose provisions is to ensure that capacity acquisitions increase consumer and total surplus. To motivate this objective, we now evaluate the impact of capacity acquisitions in the absence of use-or-lose provisions. The effect of acquisitions on consumer surplus is straightforward. Aggregate output is $Q(x) \equiv q(x) + f - x$, which is decreasing in x since $q'(x) < 1$. Therefore, in the absence of a use-or-lose provision, any capacity acquisition by an unconstrained dominant firm will reduce consumer surplus. For instance, if the dominant firm is more efficient than the fringe, consumer surplus will fall.

Total surplus is given by

$$TS(x) \equiv \int_0^{q(x)+f-x} P(z)dz - cq(x) - c_f[f - x]. \tag{8}$$

The derivative with respect to x is

$$TS'(x) = [P(q(x)+f-x)-c][q'(x)-1]+c_f-c. \qquad (9)$$

This yields the following proposition.

PROPOSITION 2. *In the absence of a use-or-lose provision: A) Any capacity acquisition by the dominant firm reduces consumer surplus; and B) fixing c_f, there exists $\underline{c} < c_f$ such that the dominant firm's equilibrium capacity acquisition reduces total surplus if $c \in (\underline{c}, c_f)$.*

Proof. Part A follows from the discussion in the preceding paragraph. To establish part B, first note that the dominant firm purchases a positive amount of fringe capacity if $c < c_f$ (Proposition 1). From (9), $TS'(x) < 0$ if $c_f = c < P$. More generally, $TS'(x) < 0$ if $P(q(x)+f-x)[q'(x)-1]+c_f < cq'(x)$. It follows that there exists a neighborhood, $(\underline{c}, c_f)$, such that capacity acquisitions reduce social surplus if c falls in this neighborhood. **Q.E.D.**

The importance of Proposition 2 is that there is a range of cost parameters such that the transfer of capacity to the dominant firm would be socially efficient *only if* policy authorities could mitigate the dominant firm's incentive to restrict output. This provides a motivation for use-or-lose provisions.

3 Imposition of a Use-or-Lose Provision

We now examine the impact of use-or-lose provisions in a market with a dominant firm. The focus is on the regulatory context, but we will provide applications to the antitrust context as well.

3.1 Use-or-Lose Provisions in the Regulatory Context

The use-or-lose provision takes the following form:

Condition UL If a firm has $\tilde{k}$ units of capacity, its output must satisfy $q \geq \alpha\tilde{k}$, where $\alpha \in (0,1)$.

The UL provision requires that the firm employ at least a fraction α of its capacity.[25] Fringe firms produce up to capacity anyway, so the provision will not affect their behavior.

---

[25]The regulator observes capacities and outputs so the constraint is enforced perfectly.

The dominant firm's output now solves the following problem:

$$\max_{q \geq \alpha(k+x)} \quad [P(q + f - x) - c]\, q. \tag{10}$$

In equilibrium, the price of capacity is again the fringe's margin, $P - c_f$.

We begin with an intuitive argument showing that the dominant firm will *buy* fringe capacity when UL binds and $c = c_f$. The argument parallels that of the benchmark case, but with a different conclusion. A binding UL constraint means that the dominant firm produces $q = \alpha k$, absent any acquisition. Suppose that the dominant firm purchases one unit of capacity ($x = 1$). It will turn $q' = \alpha$ into production and take $1 - q' = 1 - \alpha$ off the market. The cost of acquiring the q' units is $(P - c_f)q' = (P - c)q'$, and the benefit from the q' units of production is also $(P - c)q'$. The cost of acquiring the $1 - q'$ units that will be held idle is $(P - c)[1 - q']$, and the benefit is $-P'q[1 - q']$, the additional revenue from the inframarginal units of output. The net effect is $-(P + P'q - c)[1 - q']$, which is greater than zero since q exceeds the unconstrained profit-maximizing quantity. Thus, there is an incentive to buy capacity when marginal costs are equal and UL binds.

The dominant firm will buy capacity unless the fringe has a sufficiently large cost advantage. This means that the dominant firm is more likely to acquire capacity when a binding use-or-lose provision is in place than when not. Rather than providing an incentive to sell excess capacity to come into compliance, the UL provision actually enhances the incentive to acquire capacity.

We now examine formally the impact of imposing and tightening a use-or-lose provision. A change of variables simplifies the analysis. Let $y \equiv \alpha(k + x) - x$ denote the "variable component" of output when the UL constraint binds and the dominant firm acquires x units of capacity. (This quantity represents the dominant firm's net impact on output.) Aggregate output is then $\alpha(k + x) + f - x = y + f$ and $x = \frac{\alpha k - y}{1 - \alpha}$. The dominant firm's profit can therefore be written as

$$[P(y + f) - c]\alpha(k + x) - [P(y + f) - c_f]x = [P(y + f) - c]y + (c_f - c)x. \tag{11}$$

The firm gets the price-cost margin on the variable component of output, with a correction for the difference in marginal cost for the capacity purchased. Substituting for x and

14

rearranging, (11) becomes

$$P(y+f)y - \frac{c_f - \alpha c}{1-\alpha}y - \frac{c - c_f}{1-\alpha}\alpha k. \tag{12}$$

We now have the capacity acquisition problem:

$$\max_{k \geq y \geq \alpha k - (1-\alpha)f} P(y+f)y - \frac{c_f - \alpha c}{1-\alpha}y - \frac{c - c_f}{1-\alpha}\alpha k.^{26} \tag{13}$$

The first-order condition for an interior solution is

$$P'(y+f)y + P(y+f) - \frac{(c_f - \alpha c)}{1-\alpha} = 0, \tag{14}$$

and the second-order necessary condition is

$$P''(y+f)y + 2P'(y+f) \leq 0. \tag{15}$$

Let

$$\phi(y, \alpha, c, c_f) \equiv P'(y+f)y + P(y+f) - \frac{c_f - \alpha c}{1-\alpha}, \tag{16}$$

and let $y(\alpha) \equiv \alpha(k + x(\alpha)) - x(\alpha)$ denote the *equilibrium* value of y. Totally differentiating (16) with respect to α yields

$$y'(\alpha) = \frac{-\phi_\alpha}{\phi_y}\Big|_{y=y(\alpha)} = \frac{\frac{c_f - c}{(1-\alpha)^2}}{P''y + 2P'} = \frac{c_f - c}{(1-\alpha)^2(P''y + 2P')}. \tag{17}$$

We now summarize how the UL constraint affects aggregate output.

PROPOSITION 3. *Imposing or tightening a binding UL constraint has no effect on aggregate output if $c_f = c$; it lowers (raises) aggregate output if $c_f > (<) c$.*

Proof. When the constraint binds, aggregate output is $\alpha(k+x(\alpha)) + [f - x(\alpha)] = y(\alpha) + f$, which changes with α at the rate $y'(\alpha)$. The denominator in (17) is negative, by the second-order necessary condition and Assumption 1, so the sign of $y'(\alpha)$ is the opposite of the sign of $c_f - c$. This shows that tightening a binding UL constraint has the stated effect. Starting from the value of α at which the constraint just begins to bind shows that imposing a constraint has the stated effect. **Q.E.D.**

When marginal costs are equal, Proposition 3 implies that $y'(\alpha) = 0$. By definition, $y'(\alpha) = k + x(\alpha) + (\alpha - 1)x'(\alpha) = 0 \Rightarrow x'(\alpha) = \frac{k + x(\alpha)}{1 - \alpha} > 0$. An immediate implication is that a tighter constraint induces more capacity acquisition.

---

[26] The upper bound on purchases is $x = f$, which gives $y = \alpha k - (1-\alpha)f$.

15

COROLLARY 1. *Suppose that $c_f = c$. Imposing or tightening a binding UL constraint raises the amount of capacity acquired by the dominant firm.*

These results can be explained by comparing the profitability of different strategies for complying with the UL constraint. Suppose that $c_f = c$. Absent a UL constraint, the dominant firm would not buy or sell capacity, so it would produce $q(0)$. Now suppose that there is a binding UL constraint, so $q(0) < \alpha k$. Consider three ways to comply with the constraint. First, the dominant firm could simply increase its output, so that $q = \alpha k > q(0)$. Second, the dominant firm could sell capacity to the fringe and then produce $q = \alpha(k+x)$. Third, the dominant firm could acquire capacity and employ this new capacity in production; that is, acquire $x > 0$ and produce q such that $q = q(0) + x = \alpha(k + x)$. The first two strategies increase aggregate output, while the third leaves aggregate output unchanged. In fact, the first two hurt the dominant firm relative to the benchmark case, while the third leaves its profit unchanged.[27] In a sense, the dominant firm buys capacity now because the cost of purchasing any given amount is lower with a binding UL constraint than without. The constraint commits the dominant firm to produce a certain amount of output, which lowers the purchase price, all else equal.

The preceding discussion means that when $c_f = c$, the dominant firm will acquire and employ enough capacity to satisfy the constraint, leaving output unchanged from the benchmark case. As α rises, more capacity must be acquired to come into compliance. Aggregate output remains at $q(0) + f$, however.

An increase in fringe marginal cost lowers the acquisition price of capacity, which equals the fringe margin. The dominant firm will then have a heightened incentive to acquire capacity, and aggregate output will drop. (Consumer surplus will drop as well.) If the fringe marginal cost falls, the capacity acquisition price rises, and the dominant firm will acquire less capacity. Aggregate output (and consumer surplus) will rise.

To explain the impact of tightening the constraint, it is again helpful to think in terms of the dominant firm choosing the variable component of aggregate output, $y = \alpha(k + x) - x$. The *effective marginal cost* of y is $\tilde{c} \equiv \frac{c_f - \alpha c}{1 - \alpha}$ (see (12)). The effective marginal cost changes

---

[27]If the dominant firm acquires x and satisfies the UL constraint, its profit from capacity acquisition is $[P(\alpha(k+x) - x + f) - c][\alpha(k+x) - x]$. Absent the UL constraint, its profit is $[P(q+f) - c]q$. The latter is maximized at $q(0)$, so the former is maximized when $\alpha(k + x) - x = q(0)$.

16

at the rate

$$\frac{\partial \tilde{c}}{\partial \alpha} = \frac{c_f - c}{(1 - \alpha)^2}. \tag{18}$$

Thus, $\tilde{c}$ is increasing (decreasing) in α if $c_f > (<) c$. For instance, tightening the constraint lowers the effective marginal cost when $c_f < c$, increasing the dominant firm's incentive to acquire capacity. Aggregate output falls in this case. It is noteworthy that tightening the constraint reduces output precisely when the dominant firm has lower production costs. The acquisition would be efficient *if* the authority could induce the dominant firm to employ enough of it. When $c_f > c$, Proposition 3 shows that a use-or-lose provision does not accomplish this objective, and it makes matters worse for consumers by inducing the dominant firm to acquire and hoard even more capacity.

Firms often become dominant precisely because they are more efficient than fringe firms. However, there are clearly situations in which the fringe firms have lower costs than the dominant firm.[28] In these cases, tightening the UL constraint benefits consumers, although it does not necessarily increase total surplus, as we show in Section IV below.

3.2 Use-or-Lose Provisions in the Antitrust Context - Partial Divestitures

When the dominant firm produces at lower cost than fringe firms, society benefits when a unit of production is transferred from the fringe to the dominant firm. However, acquisitions that facilitate this transfer also reduce aggregate output. Antitrust authorities often remedy this problem by requiring some or all of the capacity acquired through merger to be divested to (and used by) rivals.

Although merger remedies typically include assets intended to be sufficient to prevent the merger from harming consumers, in practice, divested capacity sometimes generates less output after the divestiture than it did prior to the acquisition.[29] A simple way to capture this in our model is to assume that a divesture of x units of capacity effectively increases fringe capacity by just $(1 - \lambda)x$ units, where λ measures the productivity decline in units of output from transferring capacity to the fringe.[30] A divestiture in which capacity

---

[28]Southwest Airlines likely provides an example.

[29]See the discussion and references in the introduction.

[30]We do not mean to suggest that all divestiture remedies are unproductive. See Tenn & Jun (2009) for a

becomes less productive in this sense is isomorphic in our model to a *partial divestiture* in which a fraction of the acquired capacity is divested to fringe firms. Thus, we can examine the effect of divestitures that are less-than-fully productive by studying partial divestitures of (fully productive) capacity:

Condition PD If the dominant firm acquires $x > 0$ units of capacity, it must divest $(1 - \lambda)x$ units to fringe firms, where $\lambda \in (0, 1)$.[31]

Suppose that the dominant firm has acquired $x > 0$ units of capacity from the fringe and must divest some of it. Under PD, the acquisition of x units of capacity ultimately reduces fringe capacity by just $x - (1 - \lambda)x = \lambda x$. Since the dominant firm is not otherwise constrained, its profit-maximizing output is $q(\lambda x)$, the optimal quantity in the benchmark case when it acquires λx units of capacity from the fringe. A low (high) value of λ corresponds to the divested capacity being (not) very productive.

Letting $z = \lambda x$, the dominant firm's objective function can be written as

$$\Phi(z) \equiv \pi(z) - b(z)z = [P(q(z) + f - z) - c](q(z) - z) + (c_f - c)z. \tag{19}$$

The firm's capacity acquisition problem here is isomorphic to the acquisition problem in the benchmark case with *no* use-or-lose constraint, except that the upper bound on acquisitions changes. We therefore have the following proposition:

PROPOSITION 4. *A PD constraint has no effect on aggregate output or on the allocation of output between the dominant firm and the fringe.*

Let $z^* = \arg\max_{0 \leq z \leq \lambda f} \Phi(z)$. The dominant firm will want to acquire $x^* = z^*/\lambda$ units of capacity, which is enough to reduce aggregate output to $q(z^*) - z^* + f$. (This is feasible if $x^* = z^*/\lambda \leq f$.) The intuition for this result is straightforward. The dominant firm simply adjusts its actual purchase (x) to generate its desired net purchase $(z = \lambda x)$, given the required divestiture. In particular, the divestiture fails to achieve the objective of promoting cost-saving acquisitions without the associated reduction in output. Of course, if fringe capacity is low enough or the amount divested is high enough (i.e., the productivity

---

recent counter-example. We simply wish to explore the implications of divestitures that are less-than-fully productive for the allocation and employment of capacity in a market with a dominant firm.

[31]It will not matter that capacity acquired by the dominant firm also becomes less productive since that firm will have excess capacity.

of the transferred capacity is high enough), there will be a boundary solution in which the dominant firm purchases f and does not completely undo the impact of the PD constraint.[32]

4   Total Surplus

When the dominant firm and the fringe firms have the same marginal cost, Proposition 3 implies that the UL provision does not affect total surplus. This follows because the dominant firm adjusts its capacity acquisition in response to changes in α to leave aggregate output unchanged, and the shift in production does not affect total cost. The UL provision does affect total surplus when $c \neq c_f$ since aggregate output changes, and the allocation of production across firms also matters.

When UL binds, total surplus can be written as

$$\tilde{TS}(\alpha) \equiv \int_0^{\alpha(k+x(\alpha))+f-x(\alpha)} P(z)dz - c\alpha[k+x(\alpha)] - c_f[f-x(\alpha)]$$

$$= \int_0^{y(\alpha)+f} P(z)dz - cy(\alpha) - c_f f + [c_f - c]x(\alpha), \qquad (20)$$

since $y(\alpha) = \alpha(k+x(\alpha)) - x(\alpha)$. As UL is tightened, total surplus changes at the rate

$$\tilde{TS}'(\alpha) = \underbrace{y'(\alpha)[P-c]}_{\substack{\text{Output} \\ \text{Effect}}} + \underbrace{x'(\alpha)[c_f-c]}_{\substack{\text{Production} \\ \text{Cost Effect}}}. \qquad (21)$$

Aggregate output changes at the rate $y'(\alpha)$, and this brings a benefit of $P-c$ per unit of output (the "output effect"). The dominant firm's net purchase rises at the rate $x'(\alpha)$, and it lowers production costs by $c_f - c$ per unit purchased (the "production cost effect").

The output and production cost effects may have opposite signs, making it difficult to sign the total surplus effects in general. However, it is possible to understand the forces at work when the UL constraint is just binding and the costs of the dominant and fringe firms are not too dissimilar.

By the definition of $y(\alpha)$, we have

$$y'(\alpha) = k + x(\alpha) + (\alpha-1)x'(\alpha) \Rightarrow x'(\alpha) = \frac{k+x(\alpha)-y'(\alpha)}{1-\alpha}. \qquad (22)$$

---

[32]Recall that we implicitly assumed in footnote 18 that f was large enough that there was an interior solution in the capacity acquisition game. Such an assumption may be untenable when λ is small.

19

	Low excess capacity (k < k̂)	High excess capacity (k > k̂)
DF cost advantage ($c_f > c$)	Total surplus: + Consumer surplus: -	Total surplus: - Consumer surplus: -
Fringe cost advantage ($c_f < c$)	Total surplus: - Consumer surplus +	Total surplus: + Consumer surplus: +

Figure 1: Surplus effects of tightening a just-binding UL constraint when costs are similar.

Let α^* be the value of α at which the constraint just begins to bind. Substituting (17) and (22) into (21) and evaluating at α^* yields

$$\text{sign}\left\{\tilde{TS}'(\alpha^*)\right\} = \text{sign}\left\{\underbrace{\frac{(P-c)(c_f-c)}{(1-\alpha^*)^2(P''y+2P')}}_{\substack{\text{Output} \\ \text{Effect}}} + \underbrace{\frac{(k+x(\alpha^*)-y'(\alpha^*))(c_f-c)}{1-\alpha^*}}_{\substack{\text{Production} \\ \text{Cost Effect}}}\right\}. \tag{23}$$

Suppose that $c_f \approx c$. Then, $y'(\alpha^*) \approx 0$ (by (17)) and $x(\alpha^*) \approx 0$, so the production cost effect has the same sign as $(c_f - c)$ while the output effect has the opposite sign. The sign of $\tilde{TS}'(\alpha^*)$ turns on which effect is larger in absolute value.

There is an inverse relationship between α^* and k. If the dominant firm has little excess capacity in the absence of a UL constraint, α^* will be close to 1. In particular, as the amount of excess capacity goes to zero, α^* goes to 1, and the output effect becomes negligible. On the other hand, as the dominant firm's excess capacity in the absence of a UL constraint rises, α^* becomes smaller, while the production cost effect rises. It follows from (23) that there is some value, $\hat{k}$, such that the output effect dominates if $k < \hat{k}$, and the production cost effect dominates if $k > \hat{k}$.[33]

Figure 1 summarizes the total surplus effects and also records the consumer surplus effects for comparison. A key point is that the effect of tightening the UL constraint on

---

[33]When $\alpha = \alpha^*$ and $c_f \approx c$, aggregate output is approximately $q(0) + f$, and the argument on the right-hand side of (23) is approximately $\frac{(c_f-c)}{1-\alpha^*}\left\{\frac{P-c}{(1-\alpha^*)(P''q(0)+2P')} + k\right\}$. The term in braces is increasing in k.

both consumer and total surplus depends critically on key parameters (relative costs and the dominant firm's capacity). Indeed, total surplus effects depend on both parameters. Unless a UL policy is made contingent on these parameters, the consumer and total surplus effects may be positive or negative.

The total surplus effects of PD in Proposition 4 are obvious (assuming large fringe capacity) as the constraint leaves unchanged aggregate output and the allocation of production across firms. Therefore, PD does not affect total surplus. Welfare-reducing (-enhancing) acquisitions are still welfare-reducing (-enhancing).

5   Duopoly

Many markets that are subject to use-or-lose provisions have more than one large firm producing. An airline market may have two major carriers while a pipeline may be used by several natural gas companies. In order to examine the robustness of our results, we now consider a duopoly with a competitive fringe.

Absent a UL provision, there are hoarding incentives again, but they are tempered by free-riding as each duopolist prefers that the other one acquire fringe capacity and keep it idle. With a binding UL provision, however, the effects are the same as with a single dominant firm. In particular, tightening the use-or-lose constraint may again raise or lower aggregate output and total surplus.

Suppose that Cournot duopolists face a competitive fringe. We will use the same notation as in the previous section, with all output and capacity variables indexed by i for firm $i = 1, 2$.

As a benchmark, suppose that there is no UL provision in force. Given net purchases x_1 and x_2, the fringe will produce $f - (x_1 + x_2)$, and we write firm i's equilibrium quantity as $q_i(x_1 + x_2)$. Now consider the optimal acquisitions. Let

$$\Phi_1(x_1) \equiv [P(q_1(x_1+x_2)+q_2(x_1+x_2)+f-x_1-x_2)-c_1][q_1(x_1+x_2)-x_1]+(c_f-c_1)x_1 \quad (24)$$

denote firm 1's profit from acquiring x_1 units and then producing optimally, given that firm 2 has acquired x_2 and will produce $q_2(x_1 + x_2)$.

The rate of change of firm 1's profit from capacity acquisition is

$$\Phi_1'(x_1) = [P - c_1][q_1'(x_1 + x_2) - 1] + P'[q_1'(x_1 + x_2) + q_2'(x_1 + x_2) - 1][q_1(x_1 + x_2) - x_1]$$
$$+ c_f - c_1. \tag{25}$$

Rearranging terms gives

$$\Phi_1'(x_1) = \{P - c_1 + P'q_1(x_1 + x_2)\}[q_1'(x_1 + x_2) - 1] + P'q_2'(x_1 + x_2)q_1(x_1 + x_2)$$
$$- P'[q_1'(x_1 + x_2) + q_2'(x_1 + x_2) - 1]x_1 + c_f - c_1. \tag{26}$$

At an interior maximum of the production game, the term in braces is zero. This leaves us with

$$\Phi_1'(x_1) = P'q_2'(x_1 + x_2)q_1(x_1 + x_2) - P'[q_1'(x_1 + x_2) + q_2'(x_1 + x_2) - 1]x_1 + c_f - c_1. \tag{27}$$

We can immediately see one qualitative difference between a duopoly and a market with a single dominant firm. Suppose that $c_f = c_1$ and $x_1 = 0$. We then have

$$\Phi_1'(0) = P'q_2'(x_2)q_1(x_2) < 0. \tag{28}$$

It follows that firm 1 will *sell* capacity. (By contrast, a single dominant firm will neither buy nor sell.) The duopolists will sell because each bears only part of the loss from the resulting increase in aggregate output.

Now consider a UL constraint that binds for both firms. In the capacity-acquisition stage, the firms again submit orders and trades take place at the market-clearing price for capacity.[34] Let $y_i \equiv \alpha(x_i + k_i) - x_i$. Firm i faces an acquisition problem analogous to the dominant firm problem in (13):

$$\max_{k_i \geq y_i \geq \alpha k_i - (1 - \alpha)(f - x_j)} P(y_1 + y_2 + f)y_i - \frac{c_f - \alpha c_i}{1 - \alpha}y_i - \frac{c_i - c_f}{1 - \alpha}\alpha k_i. \tag{29}$$

Letting $\phi(y, \alpha, c_i, c_f)$ denote the objective function, the first-order conditions now amount to:

$$\phi_i(y, \alpha, c_i, c_f) \equiv P'y_i + P - \frac{c_f - \alpha c_i}{1 - \alpha} = 0, \quad i = 1, 2. \tag{30}$$

---

[34]We assume that bilateral trades between firms 1 and 2 are not permitted; if they were, one duopolist could acquire all of the other's capacity. A plausible motivation for this assumption is that antitrust authorities would be more likely to block a merger between dominant duopolists than an exchange of capacity between a duopolist and a fringe firm.

Let $(y_1(\alpha), y_2(\alpha))$ denote the solution to (30), for given marginal costs. The second-order necessary condition for firm i is

$$\phi_{ii}(y, \alpha, c_i, c_f) = P'' y_i + 2P' \leq 0, \quad i = 1, 2. \tag{31}$$

Meanwhile,

$$\phi_{ij}(y, \alpha, c_i, c_f) = P'' y_i + P', \quad i = 1, 2; i \neq j. \tag{32}$$

The case of equal marginal costs is again straightforward. If $c_f = c_i$, the first-order condition simplifies as

$$P' y_i + P - c_i = 0, \quad i = 1, 2. \tag{33}$$

The firms will adjust their capacity purchases (or sales) in response to the UL constraint so as to leave aggregate output unchanged. Once again, the binding constraint makes it more likely that a dominant firm will acquire capacity.

It is helpful for the next result to assume that $P'' y_i + P' \leq 0$. This condition, which requires that demand not be too convex, is slightly stronger than the second-order necessary condition. It implies $\phi_{ii} < \phi_{ij} \leq 0$ (i.e., own effects dominate cross effects), which yields the result.

PROPOSITION 5. *If $P'' y_i + P' \leq 0$, tightening the UL constraint lowers (raises) aggregate output if the duopolists have lower (higher) marginal costs than the fringe firms.*

Proof. Differentiating the firms' first-order conditions with respect to α yields two equations in $y_1'(\alpha)$ and $y_2'(\alpha)$. Solving gives

$$y_i'(\alpha) = \frac{-(c_f - c_i)\phi_{jj} + (c_f - c_j)\phi_{ij}}{(1 - \alpha)^2(\phi_{11}\phi_{22} - \phi_{12}\phi_{21})}, \quad i = 1, 2, \ j \neq i. \tag{34}$$

The impact on aggregate output of tightening the UL constraint is therefore

$$y_1'(\alpha) + y_2'(\alpha) = \frac{-(c_f - c_1)[\phi_{22} - \phi_{21}] - (c_f - c_2)[\phi_{11} - \phi_{12}]}{(1 - \alpha)^2(\phi_{11}\phi_{22} - \phi_{12}\phi_{21})}. \tag{35}$$

Note first that $\phi_{ii} - \phi_{ij} = P' < 0$ for $i = 1, 2; i \neq j$. In addition, $P'' y_i + P' \leq 0$ implies $\phi_{ii} < \phi_{ij} \leq 0$, which gives $\phi_{11}\phi_{22} - \phi_{12}\phi_{21} > 0$. The denominator is positive, so the sign of the right-hand side is the sign of the numerator. Since $\phi_{ij} > \phi_{ii}$, tightening the constraint lowers (raises) aggregate output when both duopolists have lower (higher) marginal costs than the fringe firms do. **Q.E.D.**

This result shows that total surplus does not change when the UL provision is tightened, if all firms have the same marginal cost. As with a single dominant firm, the firms buy more capacity (or sell less) as α rises.

The welfare analysis for the duopoly case yields expressions similar to those for the dominant firm case. When the constraint binds for both firms in equilibrium, total surplus can be expressed as

$$TS(\alpha) \equiv \int_0^{y_1(\alpha)+y_2(\alpha)+f} P(z)dz - c_1 y_1(\alpha) - c_2 y_2(\alpha) - c_f f + [c_f - c_1]x_1(\alpha) + [c_f - c_2]x_2(\alpha). \quad (36)$$

As UL is tightened, total surplus changes at the rate

$$TS'(\alpha) = y_1'(\alpha)[P - c_1] + y_2'(\alpha)[P - c_2] + x_1'(\alpha)[c_f - c_1] + x_2'(\alpha)[c_f - c_2]. \quad (37)$$

Since $x_i(\alpha) = \frac{\alpha k_i - y_i(\alpha)}{1-\alpha}$, we now have

$$x_i'(\alpha) = \frac{(k_i - y_i'(\alpha))(1-\alpha) + \alpha k_i - y_i(\alpha)}{(1-\alpha)^2} = \frac{k_i + x_i(\alpha) - y_i'(\alpha)}{1-\alpha}. \quad (38)$$

It follows that

$$TS'(\alpha) = y_1'(\alpha)[P - c_1] + y_2'(\alpha)[P - c_2] + \frac{k_1 + x_1(\alpha) - y_1'(\alpha)}{1-\alpha}[c_f - c_1]$$
$$+ \frac{k_2 + x_2(\alpha) - y_2'(\alpha)}{1-\alpha}[c_f - c_2]. \quad (39)$$

The qualitative results have similarities to the results with a single dominant firm. Equation (34) tells us that $y_i'(\alpha) = 0$ if $c_1 = c_2 = c_f$, so $TS'(\alpha) = 0$ in that case. Once again, the constraint has no effect on total surplus when marginal costs are equal. When marginal costs differ, we have the same pattern of opposing effects as before, with the tradeoff for each duopolist being the same as it is for a single dominant firm. In that sense, the results are robust to the inclusion of additional firms with market power.

6   Conclusion

This paper has considered the effects of imposing a use-or-lose provision on firms in an industry with limited capacity. Forcing a dominant firm to increase its capacity utilization raises aggregate output, all else equal. However, it may also induce the dominant firm to acquire more capacity from fringe firms, in which case aggregate output may drop. This incentive must be taken into account when evaluating the effects of use-or-lose provisions in environments that permit capacity trading such as markets for airport takeoff-and-landing slots.

Absent a use-or-lose provision, the dominant firm would purchase capacity from the fringe firms only if it is more efficient than they are. Such purchases would increase total surplus *if* the dominant firm employed enough of the acquired capacity, which is what use-or-lose provisions are designed to accomplish. Use-or-lose provisions encourage the dominant firm to acquire more capacity precisely when the dominant firm's acquisition has potential efficiency benefits (i.e., when the dominant firm is more efficient). Aggregate output falls in this case. Although the effect on total surplus is not clear cut, the effect may be negative unless the dominant firm's cost advantage is sufficiently large.

Use-or-lose provisions encourage the expansion of aggregate output when fringe firms are more efficient than the dominant firm. However, the output expansion comes at the cost of shifting production from the fringe to the less-efficient dominant firm. While total surplus may rise, it does so by encouraging inefficient production.

We also find that remedying capacity acquisitions by the dominant firm via partial divestitures is ineffective. A partial divestiture can be thought of as a use-or-lose provision applied to the acquired capacity and fulfilled by the purchasers of divested assets. The reason partial divestitures are ineffective in our model is that the dominant firm will respond by purchasing enough additional capacity to offset the requirement completely.

Turning to policy implications, the FAA's objective in adopting use-or-lose provisions in 1985 was to ensure "the full utilization of slots" and a "more efficient allocation of slots ... from the competitive slot market," while "permit[ting] maximum reliance on market forces to determine slot distribution, ... minimiz[ing] the need for government intervention in the continuing allocation and distribution of slots."[35] Our results suggest that when there is a market for slots, use-or-lose provisions cannot be relied upon to provide these benefits.

---

[35]See Department of Transportation, Federal Aviation Administration, High Density Traffic Airports: Slot Allocation and Transfer Methods, Final Rule 14 C.F.R. Parts 11 and 93, 50 *Fed. Reg.* 52184, 52194 (December 20, 1985).

Although we find that use-or-lose provisions benefit consumers and raise total surplus for certain cost parameters, a regulator (e.g., the FAA) is typically not in a position to adjust its use-or-lose policy in response to changes in these parameters.

Of course, antitrust authorities may be able to address acquisitions on a case-by-case basis. Our results imply that use-or-lose provisions do not eliminate the need for such scrutiny. The results also imply that antitrust authorities are justified in taking steps to ensure that assets divested to remedy dominant firm mergers will be fully productive. If divested assets will be sufficiently unproductive, and if dominant firms recognize this, divestiture remedies may be ineffective. Since it may be difficult to guarantee the productivity of divested assets, antitrust authorities might want to block anticompetitive mergers rather than attempting divestiture remedies, absent good evidence that divestitures will restore competition.

References

Ausubel, L. and R. Deneckere, 1989, "Reputation in Bargaining and Durable Goods Monopoly," *Econometrica* 57, 511-531.

Baer, W. and R. Redcay, 2001, "Solving Competition Problems in Merger Control: The Requirements for an Effective Divestiture Remedy," *George Washington Law Review*, 69, 915-931.

Breyer, S., 1982, *Regulation and its Reform*, Harvard University Press, Cambridge, MA.

European Commission, 2005, "Merger Remedies Study," DG Competition.

Gale, I., 1994, "Price Competition in Noncooperative Joint Ventures," *International Journal of Industrial Organization*, 12, 53-69.

Gale, I. and D. O'Brien, 2001, "The Antitrust Implications of Capacity Reallocation by a Dominant Firm," *The Journal of Industrial Economics*, XLIX, 137-160.

Krishna, K., 1993, "Auctions with Endogenous Valuations: The Persistence of Monopoly Revisited," *American Economic Review*, 83, 147-160.

Motta, M., Polo, M. and H. Vasconcelos, 2007, "Merger Remedies in the European Union: An Overview," *Antitrust Bulletin*, 52, 603-631.

Papandropoulos, P. and A. Tajana, 2006, "The Merger Remedies Study–In Divestiture We Trust?" *European Competition Law Review*, 8, 443-454.

Parker, R. and D. Balto, 1999, "The Merger Wave: Trends in Merger Enforcement and Litigation," *The Business Lawyer*, 55, 351-404.

Stigler, G., 1940, "Notes on the Theory of Duopoly," *Journal of Political Economy*, 48, 521-541.

Tenn, S. and J. Yun, 2009, "The Success of Divestitures in Merger Enforcement: Evidence from the J&J - Pfizer Transaction," FTC Working Paper No. 296.

U.S. Federal Trade Commission, 1999, "A Study of the Commission's Divestiture Process," Prepared by the Staff of the Bureau of Competition.

www.ingramcontent.com/pod-product-compliance
Lightning Source LLC
Chambersburg PA
CBHW081249170526
45165CB00009B/3264